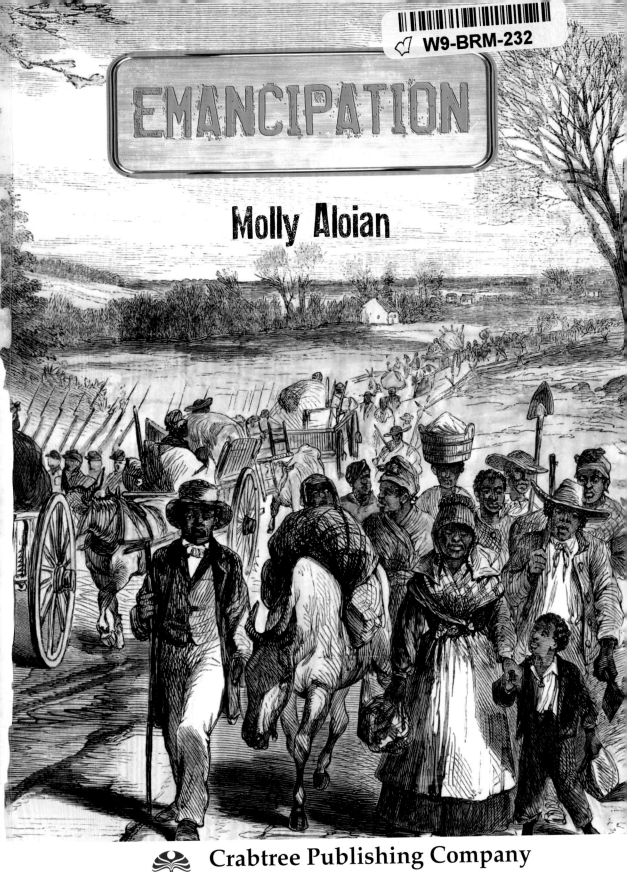

EMANCIPATION

Molly Aloian

Crabtree Publishing Company

www.crabtreebooks.com

Crabtree Publishing Company

www.crabtreebooks.com

Author: Molly Aloian
Publishing plan research and development:
   Sean Charlebois, Reagan Miller
   Crabtree Publishing Company
Photo research: Sonya Newland
Editors: Sonya Newland, Kathy Middleton
Proofreader: Crystal Sikkens
Design: Tim Mayer(Mayer Media)
Cover design: Ken Wright
**Production coordinator and prepress
   technician:** Ken Wright
Print coordinator: Katherine Berti

Produced for Crabtree Publishing by
White-Thomson Publishing

Photographs:
Alamy: North Wind Picture Archives: pp. 1,
10–11, 12, 14–15, 32–33, 36–37; **Associated
Press**: front cover; Everett Collection
Historical: p. 9; Niday Picture Library: pp.
20–21; **Corbis:** pp. 22–23; Bettmann: pp. 26–
27; Medford Historical Society Collection:
pp. 30–31; PoodlesRock: pp. 42–43; Flip
Schulke: pp. 44–45; **Dreamstime:** Julia
Freeman-Woolpert: p. 29; **Getty Images**:
pp. 8, 18, 34, 40, 41; Hulton Fine Art
Collection: pp. 6–7; Popperfoto: p. 28;
Library of Congress: pp. 3, 4–5, 13, 16, 24,
24–25, 30, 34–35, 38–39; **Shutterstock:**
BruceParrott: back cover; I. Pilon: p. 7;
Topfoto: Ullsteinbild: p. 17.

Library and Archives Canada Cataloguing in Publication

Aloian, Molly
       Emancipation / Molly Aloian.
   (Crabtree chrome)
Includes index.
Issued also in electronic formats.
ISBN 978-0-7787-1100-1 (bound).--ISBN 978-0-7787-1120-9 (pbk.)

       1. Lincoln, Abraham, 1809-1865--Views on slavery--Juve-
nile
literature. 2. United States. President (1861-1865 : Lincoln).
Emancipation Proclamation--Juvenile literature. 3. Slaves--
Emancipation--United States--Juvenile literature. 4. United
States--History--Civil War, 1861-1865--Juvenile literature. I. Title.
II. Series: Crabtree chrome

E453.A56 2013   j973.7'14   C2012-908185-X

Library of Congress Cataloging-in-Publication Data

Aloian, Molly.
   Emancipation / Molly Aloian.
       pages cm. -- (Crabtree chrome)
   Includes index.
   ISBN 978-0-7787-1100-1 (reinforced library binding : alk.
paper) -- ISBN 978-0-7787-1120-9 (pbk. : alk. paper) -- ISBN
978-1-4271-9242-4 (electronic) -- ISBN 978-1-4271-9166-3
(electronic html)
1. United States. President (1861-1865 : Lincoln). Emancipation Proclamation--Juvenile literature. 2. Lincoln, Abraham,
1809-1865--Juvenile literature. 3. Slaves--Emancipation--
United States--Juvenile literature. 4. United States--Politics
and government--1861-1865--Juvenile literature. I. Title.

   E453.A46 2013
   973.7'14--dc23
                                           2012047918

Crabtree Publishing Company

www.crabtreebooks.com   1-800-387-7650

Printed in Canada/012013/MA20121217

Published in Canada
Crabtree Publishing
616 Welland Ave.
St. Catharines, ON
L2M 5V6

Published in the United States
Crabtree Publishing
PMB 59051
350 Fifth Avenue, 59th Floor
New York, New York 10118

Published in the United Kingdom
Crabtree Publishing
Maritime House
Basin Road North, Hove
BN41 1WR

Published in Australia
Crabtree Publishing
3 Charles Street
Coburg North
VIC 3058

Contents

Slaves and Abolitionists

An Important Step

On January 1, 1863, U.S. president Abraham Lincoln took a step that changed America forever. He signed the **Emancipation** Proclamation. This official announcement freed the slaves in the southern United States.

▶ The Emancipation Proclamation was an executive order, which is an order issued directly from the president.

A Country at War

In 1863, the United States was in the middle of a bloody civil war. A civil war is a conflict between different groups in the same country. The northern states, known as the Union, were fighting the southern states, known as the Confederacy. Lincoln hoped that the proclamation would help to end the war.

Slaves were black people who were forced to work against their will for white people for no money. There were about four million slaves in the United States at the time of the Emancipation Proclamation. The proclamation freed about three million of them.

emancipation: freedom from someone else's control

5

Tense Times

Long before the American Civil War started, tensions had been building between the northern states and southern states. The North and the South were very different. In the North, there were larger cities with factories, mills, and many shops. There were also more wealthy people in the North than in the South.

▼ *Slaves were often sold at auctions. White people inspected slaves like they were animals. Then they placed their bids.*

Farmers' Fears

Most people in the South were farmers and **plantation** owners. They grew rice, tobacco, sugarcane, cotton, and other crops. Plantations required a lot of workers to farm the land. Farmers bought slaves who were forced to work in the fields, planting and harvesting crops for their masters.

PUBLIC SALE OF NEGROES.—Under the authority of a decree of the Circuit Court of Albemarle county, pronouced in the case of Michie's administrator and others, on the 30th day of October, 1855, I will offer for sale, at public auction, on MONDAY, the 5th day of May next, being Albemarle Court day, if a suitable day, if not, on the next suitable day thereafter, at the Court House of Albemarle county, *Five Negroes*, of whom the late David Tichis died possessed, consisting of a Negro Woman, twenty years of age and child two years old, a woman fifty-five years old, a negro man twenty-five years old, who has been working at the slating business, and a negro man twenty-two years old, a blacksmith.— The above lot of negroes is equal to any that has ever been offered in this market.

TERMS OF SALE—Five months credit, negotiable notes with approved endorsers, with the interest added.

GEO. DARR, Commissioner.

ap24—cds

VALUABLE PROPERTY FOR SALE !—The subscriber, wishing to remove to a more Southern climate, offers for sale, his very desirable property   It is situated in one of the

▲ *This advertisement in a newspaper from 1855 announces the sale of five black slaves.*

Most slaves originally came from Africa. They were captured there and brought to America on huge ships. White people then bought them. The slaves became the property of their white owners.

plantation: a large farm where crops are grown

Black and White

By 1860, there were about four million black slaves in the United States. Men, women, and children were all slaves. If a slave woman had a baby, that child was also a slave and belonged to the farmer. White people could sell their slaves to other farmers. This split up black families.

A Hard Life

A slave's life was usually very hard. Many white farmers treated slaves badly. Slaves were forced to work long hours. They were often beaten, whipped, and chained. They did not have much to eat and drink. If slaves tried to run away, they were **punished** harshly.

Effects of the Fugitive-Slave-Law.

▲ *Slave catchers roamed the South, rounding up runaway slaves and taking them back to their owners.*

Slaves were not paid by their owners, but some hired themselves out to make money. If they saved enough, they might be able to buy their freedom. Not many slaves ever earned enough to do this, however.

punished: treated badly for doing something wrong

The Slave-Owning South

Slave labor was a very important part of the **economy** in the South. Farmers used slaves to work the land so they could sell crops and earn money. White people also made their slaves take care of their home and children. People in the South thought that each state should be able to decide if it wanted to be a "slave state" or a "free state."

▲ *These slaves are working on a cotton plantation in the southern United States.*

Freedom in the North

The North did not rely on slaves as much as the South. Slavery had already been banned in some northern states. Many people in the North did not like slavery. They felt that all humans should be free, whether black or white.

By 1860, many countries had already banned slavery. It had been made illegal in Mexico in 1810. Canada banned slavery in the 1830s. England, Spain, and France also made slavery illegal in the early 1800s.

economy: the system of making, buying, and selling goods

Stop Slavery!

Some people, called abolitionists, formed groups to try to put an end to slavery. They held meetings and gave speeches to encourage slave owners to free their slaves. Some abolitionists helped runaway slaves so they would not be caught. They hid the slaves in their homes and gave them food.

▲ *Abolitionists helped slaves escape to freedom in the northern states and Canada through a network of roads and safe houses known as the "Underground Railroad."*

Frederick Douglass

Frederick Douglass was an important abolitionist. Douglass was born a slave, but he escaped from his owners in 1838. He wanted all black people to have the same rights and freedoms as white people. Douglass was an **inspiration** to all people who wanted an end to slavery. He was even an advisor to presidents after the American Civil War.

◀ *As well as fighting against slavery, Frederick Douglass campaigned for more rights for women and Native Americans.*

"The white man's happiness cannot be purchased by the black man's misery."

Frederick Douglass

inspiration: someone who other people admire

Making Enemies

Southern farmers and plantation owners were angry at the abolitionists. They felt that their way of life was being threatened. Southerners beat and sometimes even killed abolitionists. They destroyed their printing presses. Southerners did not want abolitionists printing newspapers that encouraged freedom for slaves.

▼ *People who were in favor of slavery burned the print shop of an abolitionist called Elijah Lovejoy.*

Scared of Change

Farmers and plantation owners in the South were not the only people who hated the abolitionists. Some people in the North still supported slavery. These northerners feared that newly freed southern slaves would move to the North to find work. They could take the jobs of white people, leaving the white people **unemployed**.

Frederick Douglass started printing a newspaper in 1847. It was called *The North Star*, and it printed articles that encouraged people who were against slavery. Part of the newspaper's motto was "Truth is of no Color."

unemployed: not having a job

▲ *Crowds gather to watch Abraham Lincoln be sworn in as president in March 1861.*

President Lincoln

In November 1860, Abraham Lincoln was elected president of the United States. Lincoln was a northerner, but he was not an abolitionist. At first, he did not want to force the southern states to free their slaves. He just wanted to stop slavery from spreading to other parts of the United States.

The South Takes a Stand

People in the South were unhappy that Lincoln had become president. They were afraid that if slavery was **outlawed** in new territories, eventually it would be banned everywhere. So the South decided to take drastic action against Lincoln and his government.

◄ *In his first speech as president, Lincoln said he would not ban slavery in the southern states.*

"I have no purpose, directly or indirectly, to interfere with the institution of slavery in the States where it exists. I believe I have no lawful right to do so, and I have no inclination to do so."

Abraham Lincoln, speaking in 1861

 outlawed: made illegal

Leaving the Union

On December 20, 1860, the state of South Carolina announced that it was no longer part of the United States of America. Within six weeks, Mississippi, Florida, Alabama, Georgia, Louisiana, and Texas also **seceded** from the Union. These states formed a new country, which they called the Confederate States of America.

▼ *The "states' rights" flag is raised in South Carolina on December 20, 1860.*

The Country Divides

It wasn't long before other southern states joined the Confederacy. Lincoln had only been president for three months when Virginia, Arkansas, North Carolina, and Tennessee also left the Union. Lincoln's worst fear had come true—America had split apart. The two sides were about to go to war.

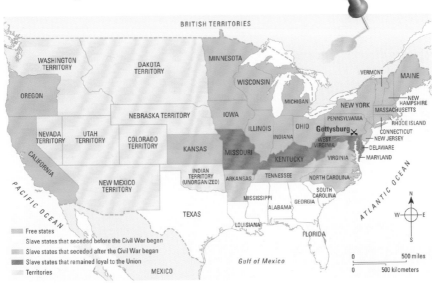

▲ *This map shows the sides that the different states were on during the American Civil War.*

"We, the People of South Carolina, have solemnly declared that the Union ... existing between this State and the other States of North America, is dissolved, and that the State of South Carolina has resumed her position among the nations of the world."

South Carolina's declaration of independence from the Union

seceded: left a group

Two Governments

The Confederacy set up its own government, separate from President Lincoln's government. The people in the South chose Jefferson Davis as their president. Davis had been a colonel in the United States Army, and he took charge of the Confederacy's war plans.

▼ *After the Confederate attack on Fort Sumter, Lincoln had little choice but to go to war.*

Attack on Fort Sumter

On April 12, 1861, the South attacked Fort Sumter in South Carolina. Fort Sumter was a Union fort. After the attack, President Lincoln had to make a difficult decision. He wanted his country to remain **united**, but he had to defend the Union by fighting against the southern states.

At first, Jefferson Davis did not think that the southern states should leave the Union. But he did think that each state should be able to make their own choice about slavery. He accepted the position of president of the Confederacy, and was its leader for the whole time it existed.

united: A group joined together as one or in agreement

▼ The American Civil War was one of the most brutal wars in history.

The Border States

Even after the Civil War began, Lincoln still did not want to ban slavery completely. He was worried that if he freed all slaves, the border states of Delaware, Maryland, Kentucky, and Missouri would join the Confederacy. These states still supported slavery, but they had stayed loyal to the Union.

Staying Together

For Lincoln, the Civil War was about keeping his country together. The United States **Constitution** said that the government should not interfere in the right of states to make certain decisions for themselves. But Lincoln also believed that America should support the idea of freedom for all people. Slavery meant that black people would never be free.

> In the four years of the American Civil War, more than 600,000 men were killed. Sometimes the battlefields were so covered with dead bodies that the soldiers still fighting could hardly see the ground.

constitution: the basic laws and beliefs of a country

Under Pressure

As the fighting moved into its second year, the war was not going well for the Union. Frederick Douglass and other abolitionists were also demanding that the president ban slavery everywhere. A respected newspaper editor named Horace Greeley **criticized** Lincoln for not setting the slaves free.

▼ *Many black men were keen to fight against the southern slave owners. This is a unit from Washington, D.C.*

▲ *Horace Greeley published articles in his newspaper, the* New York Tribune, *demanding that Lincoln abolish slavery in the United States.*

Decision Time

During this time, black men were not allowed to join the Union army. Some northerners believed that slaves should be free to fight against the Confederacy. They thought this would help the Union win the war. By July 1862, Lincoln knew he had to make a choice that would change history. Should he free the slaves?

> In April 1862, the government passed a law that freed all slaves in the District of Columbia, home to the city of Washington, the capital of the United States. It made about 3,000 slaves immediately free.

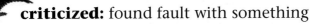

criticized: found fault with something

The Proclamation

Lincoln Writes

Lincoln thought long and hard about how to word the order that would become known as the Emancipation Proclamation. He worked on it for over a month. In July 1862, Lincoln finally finished writing. He read the proclamation to his **cabinet**. He needed to know what they thought about his decision to free the slaves.

▶ This painting shows Lincoln (third from the left) discussing the Emancipation Proclamation with his cabinet.

The Right Time

Several cabinet members supported Lincoln's proclamation. The Secretary of War, Edwin Stanton, agreed with the decision, but warned that Lincoln must choose the right time to make it public. That time came in September 1862. The Union won an important battle at Antietam Creek in Maryland. Lincoln wanted to act while people in the North felt positive about the war.

The Battle of Antietam is often called the bloodiest single day of fighting in United States history. More than 20,000 soldiers were killed or wounded during this hard-fought battle.

cabinet: a group of people who advise the president

▲ *This postcard honors President Lincoln's Emancipation Proclamation of January 1863.*

▶ *The Emancipation Proclamation was a great step toward ending slavery, but it did not make freed slaves citizens of the United States of America.*

The Final Warning

Lincoln took the first step on September 22, 1862. He announced that if the Confederate states did not return to the Union, he would free the slaves in those states. Lincoln gave the Confederacy a deadline of January 1, 1863. When no states came back to the Union, the president signed the proclamation. The slaves in the "rebel" states were free.

Freedom—But Not for All

Many people in the North were happy about the proclamation. However, it applied only to slaves that lived in places that were still at war with the Union. Slaves in parts of the country that had never left the Union, such as Maryland, Delaware, Missouri, and Kentucky, would not be set free.

"All persons held as slaves within any State or designated part of a State, the people whereof shall then be in **rebellion** against the United States, shall be then, thenceforward, and forever, free."

The Emancipation Proclamation

rebellion: a fight against authority or leaders

Signed and Sealed

When Lincoln signed the Emancipation Proclamation on January 1, 1863, it officially became law. Word spread quickly and slaves throughout the South celebrated their new freedom. But their joy quickly turned to confusion. Some southern states passed their own laws to stop slaves from leaving their owners. Were they free or not?

▲ *This slave is reading the news of the Emancipation Proclamation.*

▲ *After the proclamation, the government set up "freedman's villages" like this. Here, former slaves could get food, clothes, and go to school.*

The Meaning of Freedom

Even in places where the slaves were allowed their freedom, many of them did not know what to do. Most slaves could not read or write. When they belonged to white families, they were given food and shelter. As free people, they realized that they would have to find work, food, and homes for themselves.

On January 1, 1863, Frederick Douglass went to a special meeting in Boston that was being held to **honor** the Emancipation Proclamation. Douglass called it the "first step" in ending slavery forever.

honor: to show recognition or respect

Northern Reactions

Some northerners believed that it was wrong to free slaves only in the South. These people were against all slavery and wanted every slave to be free. On the other hand, some soldiers in the Union army felt **betrayed**. They said that they had joined the Union army to keep the country together, not to free slaves.

▼ *Many freed slaves began the long walk northward, where they hoped they would find jobs and a new life.*

Southern Reactions

Southern plantation owners were furious. Without slaves, they could not afford to run their farms. The president of the Confederacy, Jefferson Davis, felt that Lincoln had no right to free the slaves. Davis said that the Confederacy was its own country, so the United States government could not make laws for it.

> "It is the beginning of the end of the rebellion; the beginning of a new life for the nation."
>
> Horace Greeley, editor of the *New York Tribune*

betrayed: being false or disloyal to someone or something

Slaves Turned Soldiers

The Emancipation Proclamation said that former slaves were free to join the army. Many slaves were eager to fight. They also wanted to tell other slaves about the Emancipation Proclamation. These black men in the army hoped that a Union victory would mean freedom for all slaves, not just those in the Confederate states.

▼ *Eventually, more than 150,000 black men fought in the Union army. The soldiers pictured here are fighting in Virginia in 1864.*

▶ *This poster is encouraging black men to join the army.*

MEN OF COLOR
To Arms! To Arms!
NOW OR NEVER
THREE YEARS' SERVICE!
BATTLES OF LIBERTY AND THE UNION
FAIL NOW, & OUR RACE IS DOOMED
SILENCE THE TONGUE OF CALUMNY
VALOR AND HEROISM
PORT HUDSON AND MILLIKEN'S BEND,
ARE FREEMEN LESS BRAVE THAN SLAVES
OUR LAST OPPORTUNITY HAS COME
MEN OF COLOR, BROTHERS AND FATHERS!
WE APPEAL TO YOU!
STRIKE NOW!

An African American Army

By the end of January 1863, the first **regiment** of African American soldiers had been formed in Massachusetts. More were soon set up in other northern states. These regiments were commanded by white officers. But thousands of black men rushed to play their part in the battle as ordinary soldiers.

"I am a soldier now and I shall use my utmost endeavor to strike at the rebellion and the heart of this system that so long has kept us in chains."

Samuel Cabble, a slave who joined the Union army

regiment: a large group of soldiers who train and fight together

Finally Free

Lincoln Wins Again

In the North, the Emancipation Proclamation made Lincoln very popular. On November 8, 1864, he was elected as president for a second time. But the proclamation had not ended the Civil War. It just made the Confederates even more determined to save their old way of life.

▼ *People in the North thought that Lincoln was a great leader who would see the war through to the end—and a Union victory.*

Union Strength

The thousands of black men who joined the army increased the North's fighting power. There were also many more factories in the North than the South. The Union could provide its soldiers with more weapons and supplies. By the end of 1864, things were looking bad for the South.

When he was elected president again, Lincoln made a speech promising to reunite the country "with **malice** toward none; with charity for all." He said he wanted the North and the South to achieve "a just and lasting peace."

malice: hatred

The Fall of the South

Thousands of southern men had been killed in four years of bitter fighting. Also, without their slaves, farmers in the South could not produce enough food for the Confederacy. Gradually, the South grew weaker. By February 1865, the Confederate army was close to collapse.

▼ *By 1865, the Confederate army was weak and exhausted. Army leaders knew that the war was lost.*

Peace at Last

Two months later, on April 9, 1865, the Confederates surrendered. There were great celebrations across the North. People in the South realized that their lives had changed forever. They wondered how they would survive. Lincoln invited the Confederate states back into the Union and began plans to unite his country once again.

> "My **paramount** objective in this struggle is to save the Union ... If I could save the Union without freeing any slaves then I would do it, and if I could save it by freeing all the slaves I would do it."
>
> Abraham Lincoln

paramount: most important

▲ *Some states officially freed their slaves before the end of the war. This paper announces emancipation in the border state of Missouri.*

Wanting More

Even before the war ended, abolitionists were demanding more from President Lincoln. They were afraid that some people believed the Emancipation Proclamation was just a step taken to end the war. These people might think that the proclamation no longer applied when the fighting was over.

The 13th Amendment

Abolitionists also wanted freedom for all slaves in the United States, and Lincoln agreed. This meant making a new law that could never be broken. In January 1865, the U.S. Congress approved the 13th **Amendment** to the Constitution. This said that all forms of slavery were illegal everywhere in the country.

▲ *This picture shows people celebrating as the 13th Amendment is passed.*

The United States was one of the last countries in the Americas to officially outlaw slavery. The very last country was Brazil, which passed the "Golden Law" banning slavery in 1888.

amendment: a change made to an important law

*▼ Less than a week after the
Civil War ended, Lincoln was
assassinated while watching
a play at a theater
in Washington.*

Tragedy Strikes

Lincoln had fought hard to keep his
country together and win freedom
for all American people. But he did
not live to see it happen. Before the
13th Amendment was officially
passed, tragedy struck. On April 14,
1865, the president was shot by a
Confederate supporter, John Wilkes
Booth. He died early the next day.

Free at Last

When Lincoln was **assassinated**, his vice-president Andrew Johnson took over. Johnson made sure that the 13th Amendment was passed. All the slaves in the United States were free at last. The new president began the long process of rebuilding the country after years of bitterness and fighting.

Andrew Johnson was a southerner and a slave owner, but he supported the Union during the American Civil War. After the war, many people felt that Johnson did not do enough to help the freed slaves.

assassinated: killed by a surprise attack for political reasons

Paving the Way

The Emancipation Proclamation set the United States on the path toward ending slavery forever. But life was still hard for former slaves. State governments passed laws that **segregated** African Americans from white Americans. They went to different schools and ate in different restaurants. They had to travel in separate train cars.

▼ *In 1963, thousands of people—black and white—marched to Washington, D.C., to demand equal rights for African Americans.*

The Civil Rights Movement

In the 1950s, African Americans began demanding they be treated the same way as white Americans. This became known as the Civil Rights Movement. Around 100 years after the Emancipation Proclamation, the 1964 Civil Rights Act finally gave African Americans the same rights and freedoms as other Americans.

> "The central act of my administration and the greatest event of the nineteenth century."
>
> Abraham Lincoln, talking about the Emancipation Proclamation

segregated: kept apart or separate

Learning More

Books

Ben and the Emancipation Proclamation
by Pat Sherman
(Eerdmans Books for Young Readers, 2009)

The Emancipation Proclamation
by Dennis Brindell Fradin
(Benchmark Books, 2007)

The Emancipation Proclamation: Would You Do What Lincoln Did?
by Elaine Landau
(Enslow Publishers Inc, 2008)

The True Story of the Emancipation Proclamation
by Willow Clark
(Powerkids Press, 2013)

Websites

http://encyclopedia.kids.net.au/ page/em/Emancipation_ Proclamation
Encyclopedia—Emancipation Proclamation

www.rightsofthepeople.com /education/government_for_kids/ 3-5/documents/proclamation/ about.php
Ben's guide to the U.S. Government for kids

www.surfnetkids.com/go/ 69/top-ten-facts-about-the- emancipation-proclamation/
Top Ten Facts about the Emancipation Proclamation

Glossary

amendment A change made to an important law

assassinated Killed by a surprise attack for political reasons

betrayed Being false or disloyal to someone or something

cabinet A group of people who advise the president

constitution The basic laws and beliefs of a country

criticized Found fault with something

economy The system of making, buying, and selling goods

emancipation Freedom from someone else's control

honor To show recognition or respect

inspiration Someone who other people admire

malice Hatred

outlawed Made illegal

paramount Most important

plantation A large farm where crops are grown

punished Treated badly for doing something wrong

rebellion A fight against authority or leaders

regiment A large group of soldiers who train and fight together

seceded Left a group

segregated Kept apart or separate

unemployed Not having a job

united A group joined together as one or in agreement

Index

Entries in **bold** refer to pictures